VICKI COBB'S
WHY DO I DRY OFF?

STEM Kids Discover the Science of Evaporation

To the memory of
Jason Schneider

Racehorse for Young Readers books may be purchased in bulk at special discounts for sales promotion, corporate gifts, fund-raising, or educational purposes. Special editions can also be created to specifications. For details, contact the Special Sales Department, Racehorse for Young Readers, 307 West 36th Street, 11th Floor, New York, NY 10018 or info@skyhorsepublishing.com.

Racehorse for Young Readers™ is a pending trademark of Skyhorse Publishing, Inc.®, a Delaware corporation.

Visit our website at www.skyhorsepublishing.com.

10 9 8 7 6 5 4 3 2 1

Library of Congress Cataloging-in-Publication Data is available on file.

Cover and interior illustrations by John Kurtz
Cover design by Daniel Brount

Print ISBN: 978-1-63158-347-6
Ebook ISBN: 978-1-63158-351-3

Printed in China

VICKI COBB'S
WHY DO I DRY OFF?

STEM Kids Discover the Science of Evaporation

Vicki Cobb's Kid's **STEM** Play

Illustrated by
JOHN KURTZ

FOR YOUNG READERS

NOTE TO ADULT READERS

This book is designed so that your child makes discoveries. It is inquiry-driven. Questions keep the child engaged. Children love to give answers and very young children are not afraid to guess incorrectly. Reading picture books aloud to children is also a very special activity because you share an experience together. There is plenty of room for discussion around the questions and the observations. The activities are integrated into the reading, so there will be times when you stop reading and follow the directions in the book. So take your time reading. Science depends on hands-on activities, and each spread is planned to advance an important concept: evaporation is a change of state from a liquid to a gas that produces a cooling effect.

Most of the activities in the book involve evaporation and moving water from one place to another. Please have on hand the following supplies: access to water, paper towels, bath towel, a clear drinking glass, a glass bowl, a hair dryer, a ziplock sandwich bag, a small plastic cup, ice water, a refrigerator.

WIPING DRY

Wash your hands. Use a paper towel. Do you dry off?
Where does the water go?

Go for a swim or take a bath. Wrap yourself in a towel. Do you dry off?
Where does the water go?

NOT WIPING DRY

Dip your finger
in a glass of
water to wet it.

Then hold it
in the air.

Let it stay wet. Don't wipe it on anything. Don't touch anything.

Hold your hand still. Wait.

Do you dry off?

Where does the water go?

WHEN ARE YOU WET?

You are wet when water is a liquid and it sticks to you.
   Look at the water in a glass. You are looking at liquid water.

What shape is liquid water?

Pour it into a bowl.

Now what shape is it?

HOW TO KNOW A LIQUID

You can pour a liquid. It flows from one container to another container. A liquid takes the shape of its container.

It takes up space.

Its surface is flat where it meets the air.

Can you name some other liquids?
Check around your house for ideas.

Many liquids also contain water.

WHAT IS WATER MADE OF?

The smallest part of water in its natural state is a molecule. Molecules are so small no one has ever seen them. We have to imagine them.

Scientists imagine that a water molecule is made of three even smaller particles called atoms.

Each water molecule has two hydrogen atoms and one oxygen atom.
  They are arranged like the face of a mouse with the hydrogen atoms on it looking like ears.

WATER MOLECULES IN LIQUID WATER

Molecules in liquid water touch each other. They roll over each other. They form clumps and stick to each other, but the clumps are easy to break up.

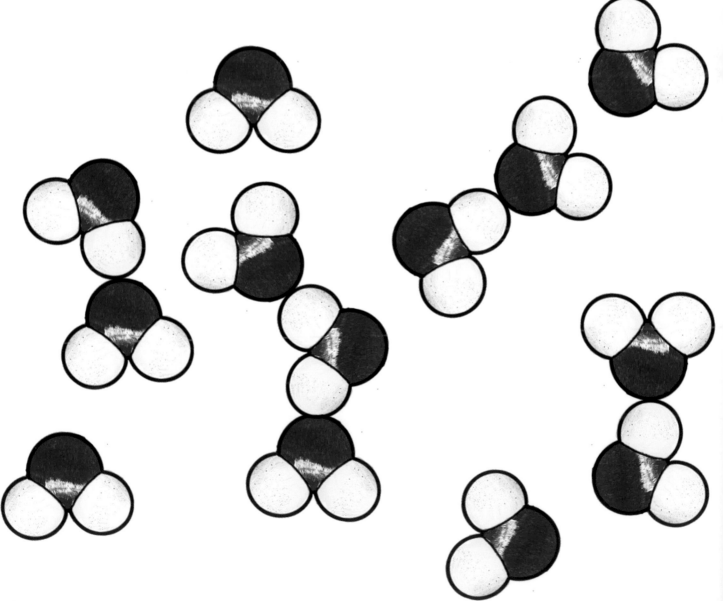

Liquid water has a skin where it meets the air. It is not a very strong skin. Want to see how the skin becomes a bag for water?

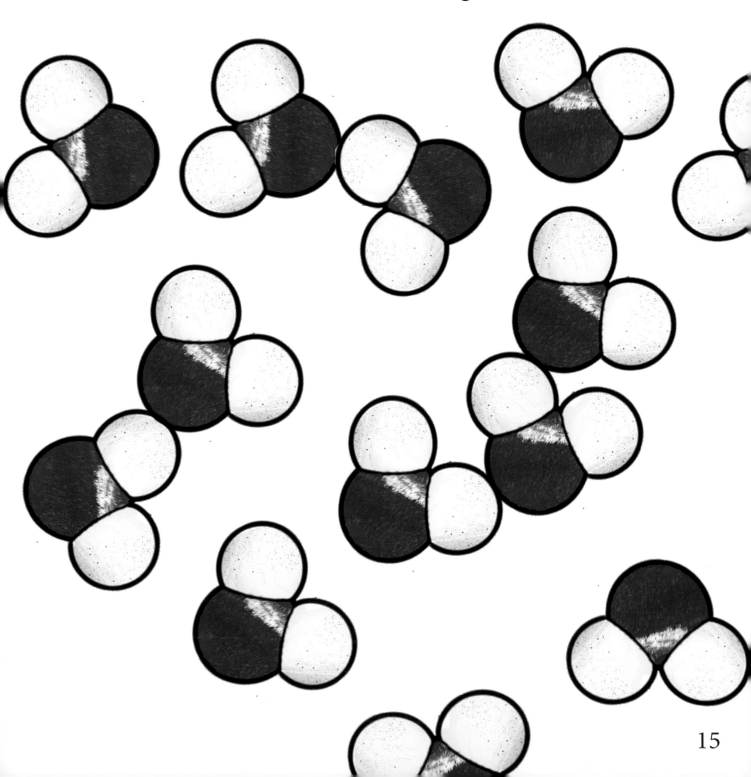

HOW TO MAKE A BAG OF WATER

Turn on the faucet. Then turn it off, but not tightly. You want it to drip very slowly. Watch closely as a water drop starts forming.

See how the drop becomes a little bag of water held together by the skin.

When the drop gets too heavy for the skin, it breaks off and becomes a **DRIP**!

Scientists observe things closely that most people take for granted.

Now you can be a scientist, too!

WHY DO YOU DRY OFF?

Wet your pointer finger again. Hold it in the air.

How does it feel? Cool?

That's because the water molecules are using heat energy from your finger to escape into the air.

That's what drying is. The liquid water is now a gas called water vapor! You can no longer see it.

WHEN WATER CHANGES TO WATER VAPOR, THAT'S CALLED EVAPORATION.

Each water vapor molecule is free to roam around in the air. On very few occasions it might bump into another air molecule.

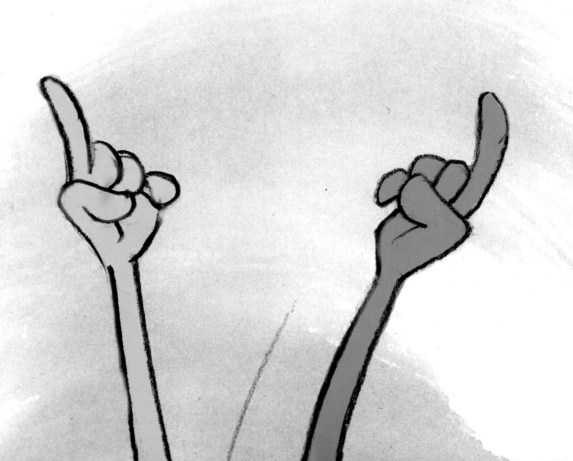

WHAT IS AIR?

Air is a mixture of gases that have no shape. Like liquids, air flows from one place to another. But this flow is called wind.

All the air molecules are very far apart. There are two main kinds of air molecules. In every ten air molecules, almost eight are a gas called nitrogen. Two nitrogen atoms stick together to make a nitrogen molecule.

The second kind of molecule is oxygen. Two oxygen atoms stick together to form an oxygen molecule.

Oxygen is the gas you breathe to stay alive.

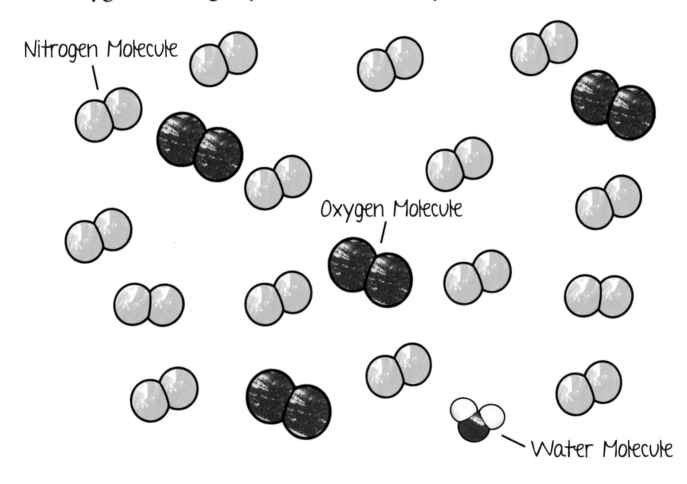

The numbers of oxygen and nitrogen and water molecules can change slightly. Air that has a lot of water in it is called humid air. Still, there are very few water molecules in air compared to all the oxygen and nitrogen molecules.

HOW DO YOU KNOW AIR IS REAL STUFF?

Air is not in a container. It is also invisible. It flows into every space that is not occupied by something else.

But it is still real and takes up space. If you can catch it you can prove it is real.

Open a zip plastic sandwich bag. Air will flow into the open bag.

Close the bag. You've caught a bag of air.

Get a small plastic or paper cup.

Try and stuff the bag of air into the cup without the bag popping open.

Bet it pushes back at you!

That push is called air pressure.

The air pressure inside you is exactly the same as the air pressure of all the air outside you. That's why you can't feel it.

23

WHAT ELSE MAKES YOU DRY FASTER?

Dip your dry finger
in the water again.
Hold it still.
   Feel how cold your
drying finger is.

Now wave it around in the air.
Does is feel even cooler?

When you wave your finger, you move air molecules, and moving air molecules are wind. Some of the air molecules crash into the water molecules on your finger and knock them into the air.

Wind speeds up evaporation.

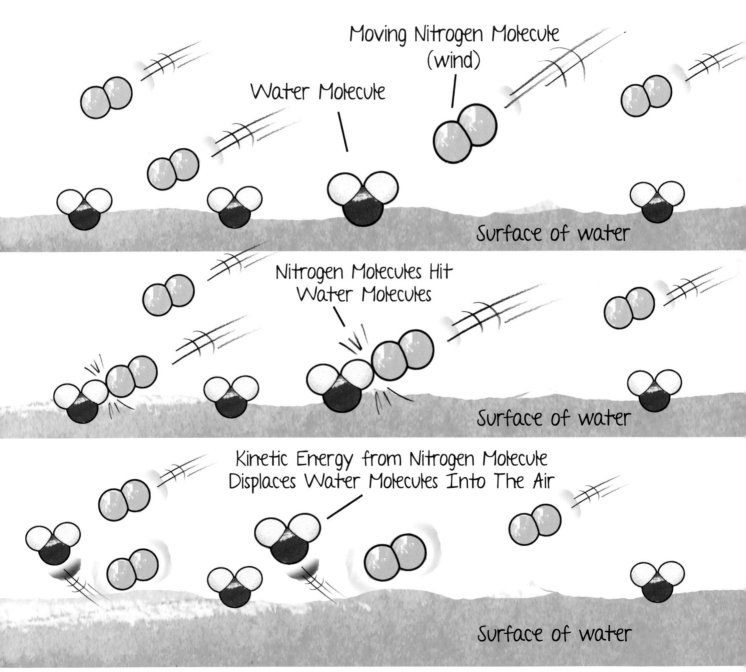

Moving Nitrogen Molecule (wind)

Water Molecule

Surface of water

Nitrogen Molecules Hit Water Molecules

Surface of water

Kinetic Energy from Nitrogen Molecule Displaces Water Molecules Into The Air

Surface of water

HOW ABOUT HOT WIND?

What's the fastest way to dry off without a towel?

Heat and wind are two kinds of energy that turn liquid water into water vapor.

Hair dryers and hand dryers in public washrooms are two inventions that dry you off quickly.

So hot wind works to dry you off twice as quickly.

Can you think of any other drying machines?

HOW CAN YOU GET WATER VAPOR OUT OF THE AIR?

If it takes heat to make water vapor, what happens when you take heat out of the air? Here's an easy way to see what happens.

Fill a glass with ice water. Soon you will see a film of water form on the outside of the glass. This is called **condensation**.

As the film continues to grow, droplets form and run down the glass. Sometimes on summer mornings you can see condensation on the grass.

That's called dew.

If the weather reporter says a cold front is coming, you might just get another kind of condensation called…

Can you guess? **RAIN**!

So, when you reverse evaporation, you get condensation.

Weather is constantly changing because of water changing from a liquid to a gas and back again.

WHAT ELSE CAN WE DO WITH EVAPORATION?

A refrigerator uses the heat in food to evaporate a liquid. This liquid is not water. It's called a **coolant**, and it's in a pipe so you can't see anything. The diagram shows how it works.

This is where the hot coolant liquid is sprayed into teeny drops in a pipe behind the back wall of a refrigerator.

INSIDE

OUTSIDE

The coolant droplets use heat from the food to become a gas, making the food cold.

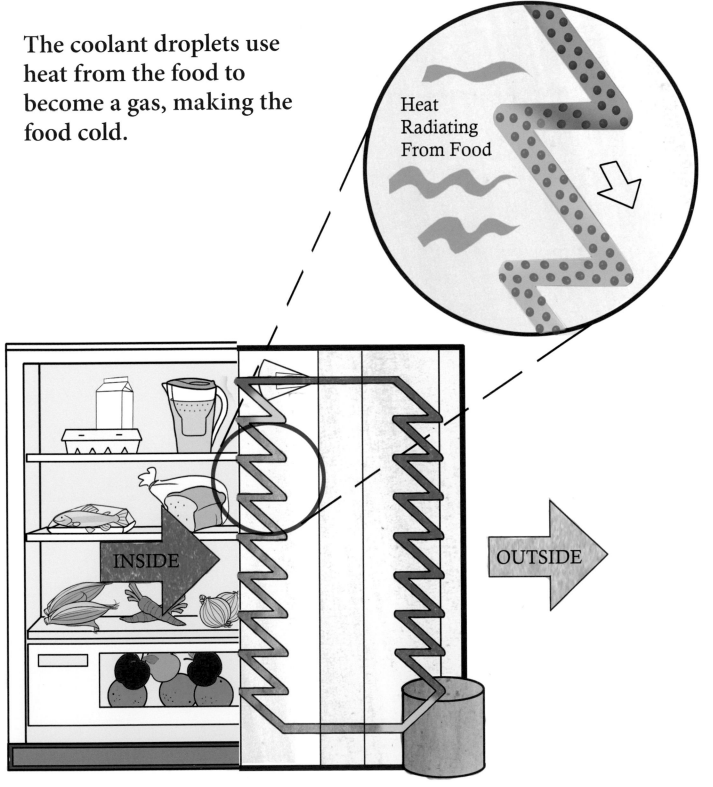

Heat Radiating From Food

INSIDE

OUTSIDE

The compressor squeezes the coolant back into a very hot gas. The coolant passes through a lot of thin pipes so it can be cooled by the air, which turns it back into a liquid.

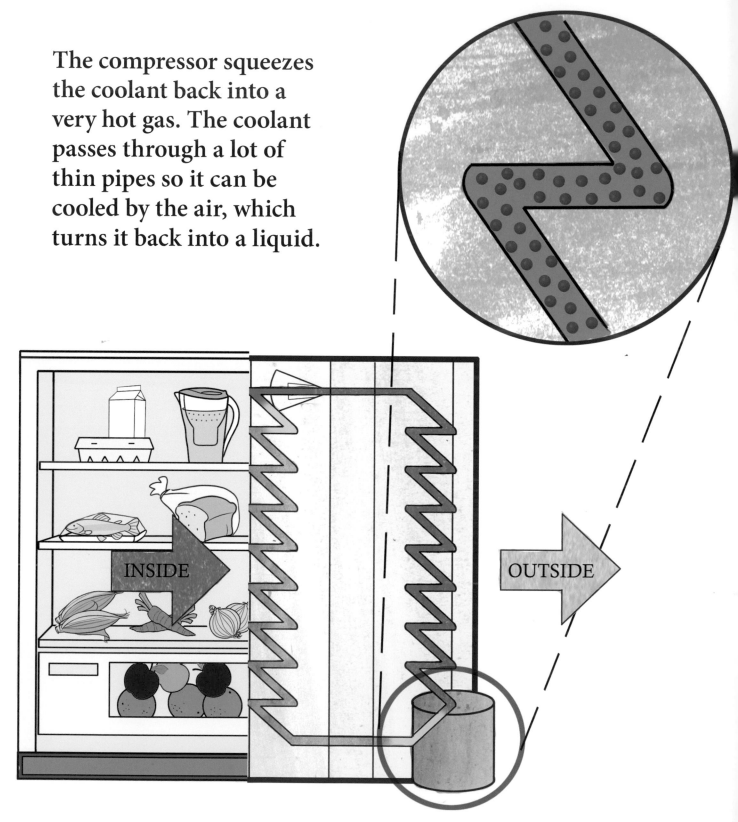

INSIDE

OUTSIDE

The hot liquid flows back into the refrigerator so it can be sprayed into droplets again and turn into a gas as it uses the heat from the food.

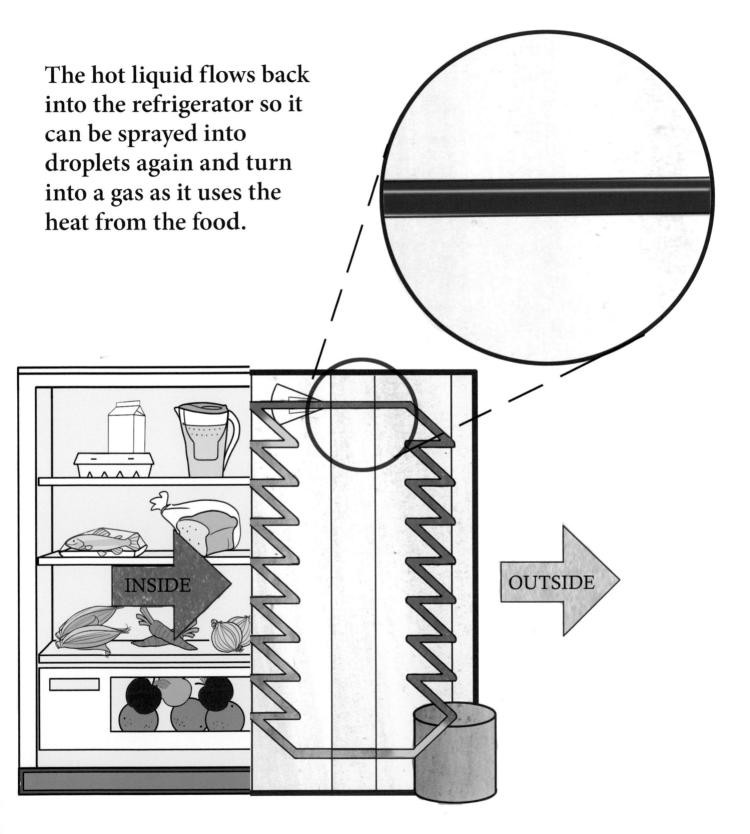

INSIDE

OUTSIDE

HOW AIR CONDITIONERS WORK

Warm Air
OUT

Cool Air
OUT

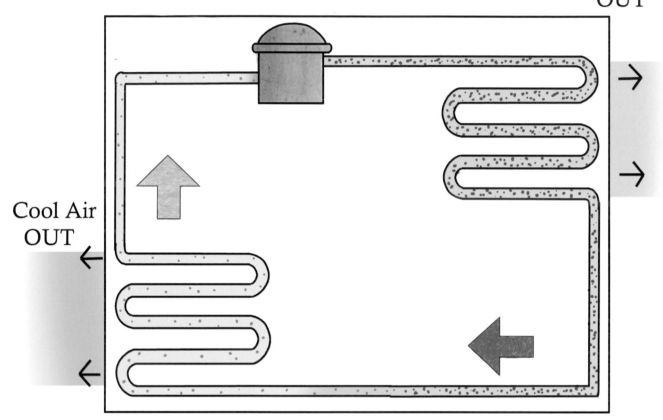

Air conditioners work the same way as refrigerators—a coolant uses the heat in the home air to evaporate, and the compressor turns it back to liquid so it can evaporate again. It all happens inside pipes.

COOLING OFF BEFORE TECHNOLOGY

You used science to see how water changes to a gas and uses heat and wind to make this change. Engineers took this idea and invented refrigerators and air conditioners.

Before there were air conditioners, people suffered through very hot days and nights. People made their own wind by fanning themselves. The fan dried peoples' skin that was moist from sweat. This cooled them off.

MAKING A FAN

1 Take a piece of paper. Fold up about an inch from the bottom.

2 Hold the bottom fold and turn the paper over.

3 Fold down about an inch from the top. Hold the ends and turn the paper over.

4 Repeat these zig-zag steps until the entire piece of paper is like a fan.

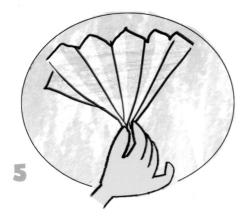

5 Hold the bottom together. The top spreads out.

6 Wave until you feel the breeze.

HOW COULD YOU SLEEP WITHOUT AIR CONDITIONING?

The nights were the worst.

Children went to bed and covered themselves with only a sheet.

Then their mothers took a bottle of water with a sprinkler on top, like a watering can, and made the sheet damp.

The water on the sheet used the heat from each child to evaporate. As the sheet dried, the children became cool enough to sleep.

Evaporate

Evaporate

Evaporate

MORE TO DISCOVER

Here are some other questions where you can make discoveries.

Do other liquids evaporate? How about perfume? Open a bottle of perfume. You can smell it only when the scented molecules go into the air and reach your nose.

You might be interested in discovering your sense of smell by reading a book about it.

There are warm places around cooling machines like air conditioners and refrigerators. See if you can feel the warm air coming off them.

A BONUS EXPERIMENT

Imagine how much water evaporates from the surface of the ocean. Water vapor rises and makes clouds. Water vapor becomes rain drops, which fall back into the ocean. This is called the water cycle because it keeps going around and around forever. Have you ever tasted the ocean? Have you ever tasted rain?

The ocean is salty. Rain is not. What happens to salt when water evaporates? Do an experiment to find out.

Measure out four tablespoons of water into a small cup. Add a half teaspoon of salt. Stir well until you can't see any salt in the water. Taste the water. Is it salty?

Pour the saltwater into a dark-colored saucer and put it on a window sill. Wait until all the water has evaporated and the saucer is dry. What do you see in the saucer? Taste it to make sure.

You've just made a scientific discovery! You've answered the question, "What happens to the salt in the ocean when water evaporates?"

STEM
WORDS
GLOSSARY

AIR: a mixture of gases that surround the Earth. It is invisible, and you can't smell it or taste it. But you can feel it when it moves, and you can see how moving air can make other things move. We live at the bottom of a sea of air.

ATOM: the smallest particle of all matter. Atoms of one kind of material combine with other atoms to form something completely different. So the atoms of hydrogen and oxygen, both gases, combine to form water, which is a mostly a liquid on the surface of the earth.

COMPRESSOR: a machine that squeezes air or other kinds of gases. In a refrigerator, the compressor squeezes a liquid called a coolant. It squeezes the cold coolant gas so that it gets hot. The hot gas leaves the compressor and travels through many coiled tubes that allow the heat to escape to the air.

CONDENSATION: the change of a gas to a liquid. Water vapor in the air condenses to form rain, dew, snow, sleet and other forms of liquid or frozen water. It is part of the water cycle.

COOLANT: a liquid that is used in refrigerators and air conditioners. It absorbs heat from air or food so that they cool down. It is then compressed to that it can release the heat someplace else. In a refrigerator, the heat goes into the air in the kitchen. In an air conditioner, the heat is released to the outside air.

DEW: liquid that condenses on cool objects from water vapor in the air. It also forms on the outside of a glass of an iced drink on a hot summer day.

EVAPORATION: the change of liquid water to water vapor—a gas. It happens wherever liquid water touches air. The water can be on the surface of an ocean, lake or river. It can be on your skin. It happens everywhere. Water takes heat from air or your skin to become water vapor. As a result, your skin feels cooler.

EVAPORATOR COILS: metal tubes that contain a coolant. Engineers use them wherever they need to make things cold. Inside the coils there is a gas that changes into a liquid as it removes heat from air in a refrigerator or air conditioner.

EXPANSION VALVE: a device inside a refrigerator or air conditioner that takes hot liquid coolant and sprays it into a small space where it becomes many small droplets. The coolant droplets that leave the expansion valve are now ready to absorb heat from food or air and become a gas.

HEAT: a form of energy that changes liquid water into water vapor.

HYDROGEN: a gas that becomes two parts of a water molecule. It is the lightest gas in the universe.

LIQUID: any material that can be poured, can flow from one place to another, and is flat where it meets the air. Water is the most common liquid on earth.

MOLECULE: the smallest particle of any material that has all the properties of that material. A water molecule is made of two atoms of hydrogen and one atom of oxygen.

OXYGEN: one of the gases in the air. It is the most important to use, because oxygen is the gas we need to breathe into our bodies in order to stay alive.

RAIN: a form of condensation of water vapor in the clouds that is heavy enough to fall to earth.

WATER: a colorless, odorless liquid when the temperature is between 32°–212° F (0°–100° C). The lower temperatures are when water freezes to become ice, a solid. The higher temperatures are when water boils and changes into a gas. F stand for Fahrenheit and C stands for Celsius. They are two different systems for measuring temperature using a thermometer.

WATER VAPOR: a gas of water molecules that have evaporated into the air. Water vapor acts like the other gases in the air. You can't see it unless it condenses into a cloud that is made of liquid water droplets. Humidity is the name we give to the water vapor in the air. Warm air can become much more humid than cooler air.

WATER CYCLE: the constant change of water on Earth from a liquid to water vapor (evaporation) and back to a liquid again (condensation).

WIND: moving air. In weather, wind is caused as colder air moves into warmer air. Sometimes this causes rain as the cooler air makes water condense out of the warmer air.

MORE VICKI COBB BOOKS
FROM RACEHORSE FOR YOUNG READERS